DATE DUE

IN THE SPANISH WEST

HOW WE LIVED...

IN THE SPANISH WEST

by R. Conrad Stein

BENCHMARK BOOKS

MARSHALL CAVENDISH
NEW YORK

ACKNOWLEDGMENT

*For his generous assistance and expert advice, the author wishes to thank
Clarence G. Seckel, Jr., Curriculum Coordinator in the Social Studies,
East Saint Louis School District 189, East Saint Louis, Illinois.*

Benchmark Books
Marshall Cavendish Corporation
99 White Plains Road
Tarrytown, New York 10591-9001

• • •

Library of Congress Cataloging-in-Publication Data
Stein, R. Conrad
In the Spanish West / R. Conrad Stein
p. cm—(How we lived)
Includes bibliographical references and index.
Summary: Describes various aspects of the life of early settlers in the Spanish
West including their relations with Indians, farming and ranching, trading,
religion, and the importance of community.
ISBN 0-7614-0906-8 (lib.bdg.)
1. Spanish Americans Southwest, New—History—16th century—Juvenile literature.
2.. Pioneers Southwest, New—History—16th century—Juvenile literature.   3. Frontier and pioneer life—
Southwest, New—Juvenile literature.   4. Southwest, New—History—To 1848—Juvenile literature.   [l. Pioneers.
2. Frontier and pioneer life—Southwest, New.   3. Southwest, New—History—To 1848.]   I. Title.   II. Series.
F790.S75S84   2000   98-24087   979'.00468—dc21   CIP   AC

• • •

Printed in Hong Kong
1 3 5 6 4 2

• • •

Book Designer: Judith Turziano
Photo Researcher: Debbie Needleman

• • •

PHOTO CREDITS

Front cover: Courtesy of Jack Parsons; page 2: New York Public Library / Art Resource, NY;
pages 6–7: George H. H. Huey; pages 8–9: Mural by Gerald Cassidy, Courtesy of Museum of New Mexico,
Neg #20206; page 11: Harald Sund / The Image Bank; pages 14–15: Photo by Philip Harroun, Courtesy of Museum of New Mexico,
Neg #12534; pages 16, 56: Robert Frerck / Odyssey Productions / Chicago; pages 18, 19: Jack Parsons; pages 24–25, 36:
Stock Montage; page 26: Museo de America, Madrid, Spain / Bridgeman Art Library, London / New York; pages 30–31:
The Newberry Library / Stock Montage; page 32: Underwood & Underwood / Corbis; pages 34–35, 41, 44–45, 46, 50, 57:
North Wind Picture Archives; pages 38–39: Santa Barbara Mission Archive Library; page 43: Photo by Helen Sosaya, Courtesy of
Museum of New Mexico, Neg #123136; page 48: National Museum of American Art / Art Resource, NY; pages 54–55: Daughters
of the Republic of Texas Library, Yanaguana Society gift; page 59: Christie's Images / London, UK / Bridgeman Art
Library London / New York; page 62: Paul Chesley / Photographers Aspen

Contents

America's First Pioneers 6

❖**1**❖

The Spanish West: New Spain's Northern Frontier
9

❖**2**❖

Life and Work in a Lonely Land
15

❖**3**❖

Growing Up in the Spanish West
25

❖**4**❖

The Church: Foundation of the Spanish West
35

❖**5**❖

The Spanish West Community
45

❖**6**❖

Light and Twilight of the Spanish West
55

Glossary **63** • The Spanish West in Time **64**
Places to Visit **65** • To Learn More about the Spanish West **67**
Bibliography **68** • Notes on Quotes **69** • Index **70**

Map of New Spain **12**

America's First Pioneers

For generations we have been taught that our country's history started in 1620. That year the Pilgrims sailed on the *Mayflower* and established a settlement at Plymouth Rock in Massachusetts. For centuries the people of the United States have looked upon the *Mayflower* and Plymouth Rock as proud symbols of their national origin.

But more than twenty years before the Pilgrims' voyage, Spanish-speaking people had begun to colonize the southwestern part of our nation. These pioneers came from Mexico. After a long journey north, they discovered wild and beautiful lands. They settled down and built farms, ranches, and small villages. They gave their new lands names: Texas, New Mexico, Arizona, California.

The Spanish settlers were the first Europeans to establish permanent roots in what is now the United States. They were America's first pioneers.

Spanish horsemen make their way across the countryside. This painting was done by Navajo artists on the wall of a canyon in present-day Arizona.

❖1❖
The Spanish West: New Spain's Northern Frontier

*"It is, no doubt, the best land in all these [Americas].
Indeed, the land needs no circumstance to make it blessed."*

—CABEZA DE VACA, A SPANISH EXPLORER,
*upon seeing the lands of Texas and New Mexico in
the 1530s. He may have been the first European
to see the Spanish West.*

The people who journeyed north from Mexico to the Southwest belonged to New Spain, part of the great Spanish Empire. They were subjects of the Spanish king, whose possessions included lands in not only North and South America, but around the globe.

In 1519, about eighty years before these pioneers set out, Spanish conquistadors had landed on the shores of Mexico. Within two years they had defeated the native people, the Aztec Indians. Before long, more Spaniards crossed the Atlantic Ocean and settled down. In time some of these colonists ventured north. By 1598 the first settlement had been made in what is now the state of New Mexico. As more colonists moved north, the land they claimed became New Spain's northern frontier—the region known in history as the Spanish West.

Colonists in the Spanish West spoke the Spanish language and swore loyalty to the king of Spain. They played guitars and danced lively Spanish fandangos. But the colonists learned from the Native Americans how to live off the land. Their staple food was the Indian corn cake, which the Spaniards called a tortilla. For a treat the people ate chopped meat wrapped in a roll of cornmeal dough, a tamale. Many colonists of the Spanish West mastered Indian languages and married into Indian families. They visited Indian doctors when they were sick. The people lived with feet in two worlds—Spanish and Indian.

New Spain's northern frontier was a vast and lonely territory. It touched upon parts of present day Oklahoma, Colorado, Utah, and Nevada, although almost no Spaniards lived in those outlying areas. Even after many years of settlement, the northern frontier held few colonists. By 1800, in fact, there were only about 40,000 people of Spanish blood.

The land itself was beautiful as well as hostile. Spaniards wrote with wonder about California redwood trees that rose taller than cathedrals. In the grasslands of Texas, the Spaniards gazed at herds of buffalo so thick they blackened the ground.

Much of the Spanish West, however, was home only to cactus plants and swirling desert sands. Colonial farmers prayed for rain. Then, all

CORONADO, EXPLORER OF THE SOUTHWEST

In 1540 Francisco Vásquez de Coronado led an army of Spaniards and Indians out of Mexico and into the unexplored areas to the north. He hoped to find cities holding treasures of gold. Twenty years earlier the Spaniards had plundered great quantities of gold from the Aztecs in Mexico. Coronado's soldiers were so excited over the prospects of getting rich that they called the region to the north *un nuevo Mexico*, "a new Mexico." Thus the area and later the American state got their name. Coronado found no treasure, but his soldiers were the first Europeans to see the spectacular Grand Canyon of Arizona.

The Grand Canyon

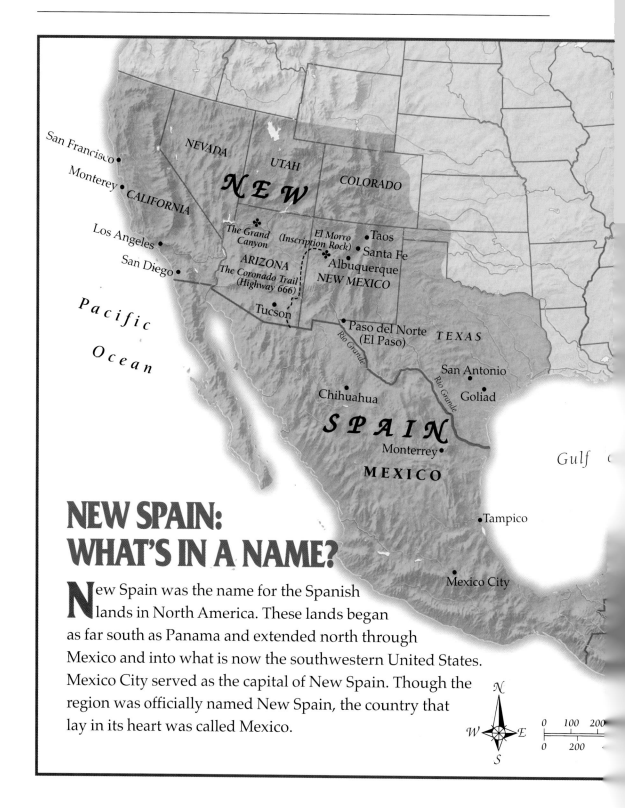

NEW SPAIN: WHAT'S IN A NAME?

New Spain was the name for the Spanish lands in North America. These lands began as far south as Panama and extended north through Mexico and into what is now the southwestern United States. Mexico City served as the capital of New Spain. Though the region was officially named New Spain, the country that lay in its heart was called Mexico.

co

Atlantic

Ocean

Caribbean

Sea

es

© Oxford Cartographers

too often, killer storms lashed out of the heavens. The storms were laced with hailstones so large they dented the helmets of Spanish soldiers.

Violence was also part of the landscape. Native Americans of the region looked upon the Spaniards as invaders. Furious wars broke out between the colonists and the original inhabitants.

Despite these difficulties the Spaniards farmed the land, worshipped God, and genuinely enjoyed life. How did the colonists live in the lovely but rugged frontier? This is the story of the people of the Spanish West, America's first pioneers.

✧2✧
Life and Work in a Lonely Land

"The region farthest north, which forms a separate frontier, is that of New Mexico, whose remote province is isolated and alone, but has sufficient strength in its many towns and the good quality of its inhabitants."

—A LETTER WRITTEN BY A GOVERNMENT OFFICIAL
OF NEW SPAIN IN THE LATE 1700S

THE ADOBE FRONTIER

The men and women who came to the northern frontier included white-skinned Spaniards, dark-skinned Indians from Mexico, and members of a new race called mestizos (meh-STEE-zohs). The mestizo race was created in Mexico through the intermarriage of Spanish and Indian people.

The walls of this adobe house in Santa Fe, New Mexico, were built by Native Americans in the 1300s. The house is said to be the oldest in the United States.

Today more than 90 percent of the Mexican people are mestizos. But when colonists first moved north, mestizos were a minority. Mexico was then ruled by white Spaniards. The Spaniards restricted mestizos from owning land and operating businesses. In the northern frontier, however, discrimination against mestizos faded and the race thrived. By the early 1800s the vast majority of people in the Spanish West were of the mestizo race.

If one word could describe the lifestyle of the northern frontier, that word would be isolation. New Mexicans, for example, lived a six-month wagon journey from their capital in Mexico City. A trip to Chihuahua, the nearest settlement in northern Mexico, took two months. Isolation forced the settlers to develop a special way of life, one tailored to this beautiful but rugged region.

The Spaniards built their houses of adobe, a material provided by the land. Adobe is a sun-dried brick. It is made from wet clay, which workers kneaded with their bare feet until it was a little thicker than oatmeal. They then added straw as a binder, shaped the clay into bricks, and let the bricks dry in the sun. When properly maintained, an adobe wall will stand for many generations. People in New Mexico today live in adobe houses whose walls were first built by Spaniards hundreds of years ago.

For maintenance, the outside walls were covered with a layer of clay every few years. The clay was spread on by women. It was thought that women had the dainty hands and superior patience to get into every nook and corner of the outside wall. For ages Native American people had been building adobe houses in the Southwest. Plastering the outside walls was considered a women's chore in Native American cultures also.

The colonists reinforced their adobe walls with wooden beams. The beams, called vigas (VEE-guhs), came from pine trees, which were cut and hauled down from mountaintops. Vigas supporting the roof often protruded over the front of the house, giving it a pleasing look. Poor families built small houses, but an adobe home could be easily expanded when the owner had spare money. A priest's house in Taos, New Mexico, grew from two rooms to twenty-one rooms over the course of fifty years.

Conditions inside the houses were sparse. Wooden floors were almost

Houses in the Spanish West were simply furnished.
The banco in the corner, covered with a blanket, served as a bed.
The rug on the dirt floor provided a place to gather for meals or
prepare food. There were few iron utensils. People made most
of their household tools from clay or wood instead.

unknown. People walked and slept on dirt floors, which were tamped, or pressed, hard. In New Mexico the dirt floors were covered with rugs made from sheepskins. Window glass was rare. Windows were made of a local mineral called selenite, which barely allowed the passage of light.

Furniture was simple or even nonexistent. Instead of a sofa, families sat on an adobe bench called a *banco*. The *banco* was built into the wall. Bedding consisted of blankets unrolled and spread on the floor at night, and then rolled up again in the morning. There was no such thing as a dining room table. Families ate squatting on the floor. They held their plates, picnic style, on their laps.

Although the colonists lived with few wooden furnishings, they created minor masterpieces in wood. The wooden storage chest was a prized possession in a New Mexican house. It usually stood on built-in legs. The chest held blankets, perhaps some china-ware, and a few treasured silver or gold coins. No mere box, the family chest was leather-covered, or it was adorned with carvings.

Churches were graced with masterfully carved and gaily painted statues of the saints. Craftsmen who fashioned the wooden creations were called

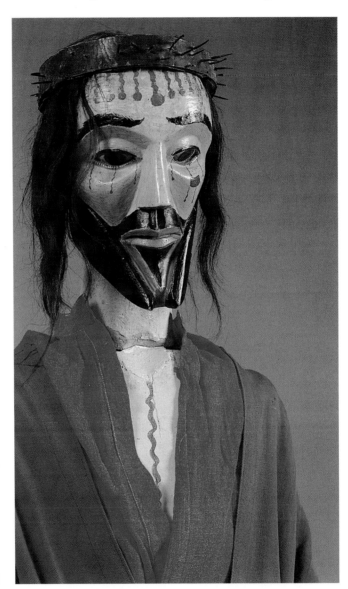

Santeros *made their figures look as realistic as they could, often by adding real hair and glass eyes. This statue of Christ once stood in a Spanish West church.*

santeros. The *santeros* gave their figures glass eyes and real hair, which they cut off their own heads. So intense was the work of the santeros that their statues seem to emerge with individual personalities, like living men and women.

COOKING: A WOMAN'S WORLD

Outside each New Mexican house stood a beehive-shaped adobe oven. There women built wood fires and baked bread and delicious cakes. Women of the Spanish West had few rights. They could not become leaders in government or in the church. But when it came to food preparation, the woman of the house was boss.

Women were hampered in their work by a frustrating shortage of iron. Iron pots were so rare that they were passed down like heirlooms, mother to daughter. Clay pots were found in all kitchens. Some had delicate designs or fancy painting on the outside. Spoons were made from wood or from animal bones. Dinner plates were fashioned from wood. Gourds served as water glasses. A lack of iron plagued all industries in the Spanish West. Even plowshares were made of wood.

Women of the Spanish West made delicious meals with the materials they had at hand. New Mexico was a sheep-ranching region. New Mexican women made tasty stews of mutton, beans, and vegetables. Throughout the Spanish West, beans were a part of almost every meal served. Most households also kept chickens and pigs. Bacon and fried eggs was a special breakfast prepared for holidays.

The corn tortilla was the common bread of the Spanish West. The colonists grew wheat and barley, but corn was their staple crop. A Spanish priest in New Mexico once said, "Here corn is God." To make tortillas, women ground corn to a mush, patted the mush into thin cakes, and baked them. A stack of tortillas was served with all meals. Tortillas even made up for the lack of eating utensils caused by the iron shortage. During meals people scooped up the food in a tortilla and then ate it, tortilla and all.

People in the Spanish West flavored their meals with chili peppers.

Cooks crushed the peppers with a little water and created a sauce that was tasty as well as fiery. A simple test of chili sauce applied: the hotter the better. If a guest wished to compliment a woman's

A TASTE OF THE SPANISH WEST

Enchiladas were served in the Spanish West and are enjoyed in the United States today. Here is a simple recipe for chicken enchiladas that uses items available in most supermarkets.

CHICKEN ENCHILADAS

8 tortillas
1 teaspoon olive oil (optional)
$1/2$ pound cooked chicken, stripped from the bone and cut in small chunks
1 can (8 ounces) tomato sauce or enchilada sauce
$1/4$ pound mozzarella cheese, shredded
1 can (8 ounces) chopped chili peppers or chili sauce (optional)

First preheat the oven to 400 degrees Fahrenheit. Then warm the tortillas one by one over the burner of the stove, or fry them slightly in a teaspoon of olive oil. You might want to ask an adult to help you at the stove. The tortillas must be warmed or they will crack when you try to roll them. Spoon the cooked chicken onto the tortillas, roll them into sausagelike shapes, and line them up in a lightly greased baking dish. Cover the tortillas with tomato sauce or enchilada sauce. Then sprinkle shredded mozzarella cheese over your creation. Bake about fifteen minutes, or until the cheese is melted and the sauce is bubbling. Finally, if you are brave, add some zest to your dish by putting a spoonful of chopped peppers or chili sauce on top. Don't add too much, especially if you are unfamiliar with peppers. Too much will set your mouth on fire.

cooking, he or she said, "My, this sauce would raise the dead."

SIMPLE CLOTHES FOR AN UNHURRIED LIFESTYLE

Most people in the Spanish West had only two outfits—one to wear to church or to parties, another for working in the house or the fields. For everyday use a woman wore a cotton dress with long sleeves. Spanish colonists loved bright colors. Women usually sewed brilliant red-and-yellow stripes on their clothes. Rarely did women wear hats. In the cold weather they wrapped their heads in a wool scarf called a rebozo, which doubled as a pack to carry a tiny baby.

The unmarried woman's treasure was a party dress, which she hoped would attract the eye of a man. Such prized dresses were bought during rare visits the woman made to a northern Mexican town. One popular dress worn only on special occasions was called a "half-step." The dress was so long and fitted so tightly at the ankles that it permitted the young woman to take only half a step at a time.

Men at work on the ranches often wore long trousers made from deerskin. Leather vests were also widely used. Silver was a fairly common metal. It was used for buttons on vests and for flashy sequins on both men's and women's clothing. A woolen cloak called a serape (suh-RAH-pee) was favored by men. The serape looks like a blanket with a slit in the middle. Men poked their heads through the slit and let the sleeveless serape trail down to their knees. Men also wore straw hats with wide brims called sombreros.

Dapper young men valued one special suit of clothes, which they purchased on a trip to Mexico. The outfit was reserved for gala events such as a village dance. The most stylish aspect of the suit was a pair of pants called calzones. The pants had split seams running down each side, which were held together with a line of silver buttons. Before going to the dance, the young man polished the silver buttons till they sparkled.

Men and women of the Spanish West lived an unhurried life. Their patterns changed with the seasons—winter and summer—rather than by the day. In the late 1700s a resident of Spanish Texas looked back upon his youth and said, "We were of the poor people. . . . To be poor in those days meant to be very poor indeed, almost as poor as the Savior in His Manger. But we were not dissatisfied. There was time to eat and sleep and watch the plants growing. Of food we did not have overmuch—beans and chili, chili and beans."

NEW MEXICO, MOTHER OF SPANISH WEST REGIONS

New Mexico was the first region settled by Spanish colonists. And it was by far the most populous region of the northern frontier. Its first colonists came in 1598, led by an official named Juan de Oñate. Twelve years later another group of colonists founded Santa Fe, which became New Mexico's capital. Settlers to New Mexico clustered along the upper Rio Grande. Albuquerque, founded in 1706, was a major village. By the early 1800s New Mexico held about 30,000 Spanish colonists.

◇3◇
Growing Up in the Spanish West

The Hummingbird tells me
Not to look for love,
But to continue as she does,
Sipping the flowers.

—A SONG FAVORED BY YOUNG GIRLS
IN OLD NEW MEXICO

EDUCATION

There were no schools as we know them in New Spain's northern frontier. If a rich man wanted his son to learn reading and writing, he sent the boy to a priest for lessons. It was supposed that a girl's future lay in the home and in the kitchen. A boy, on the other hand, could aspire to a government job or to the priesthood. Because priests had to be paid to teach their students, only well-to-do families educated their sons. The vast majority of other people lived their entire lives unable even to sign their own names on a piece of paper.

The colonists had strong religious beliefs. Nearly all the people were

A wealthy Spanish West family

Roman Catholics. The church was the fabric that held their society together. Important religious ceremonies, known as sacraments, marked a person's passage through life, from infancy to death. Priests were powerful community leaders as well as teachers.

The biggest day in the life of a boy or girl was his or her first Holy Communion. A colorful Mass honored first communicants, who were usually ten years old. After the religious service the communicants paraded to the house of the nearest classmate. There they ate a huge breakfast of eggs, beans, and tortillas. Singers and musicians playing violins and guitars serenaded them.

To the children's astonishment, older cousins and uncles now addressed them as *senor* and *senorita*, "mister" and "miss." In the Holy Communion ceremony, called the Eucharist, they had received the sacred bread and wine, the Body and Blood of Christ. This meant they were now adults in the Catholic community. After breakfast the communicants were marched to the next house for another enormous breakfast. By the time they reached the eighth or tenth house, they were stuffed to the bursting point. None would forget their first Holy Communion.

Priests often employed children as actors in special plays they created. The plays were designed to give Bible lessons to colonists as well as Native Americans. A popular play told the story of Adam and Eve. It was performed outdoors. Props included a carved wooden figure of the Tree of Good and Evil. The play was given in pantomime so that both Spanish and Indian people could understand its meaning. The highlight came when a young girl, the Eve figure, offered Adam an apple from the forbidden tree. With exaggerated motions—almost like the gestures of an actor in a silent movie—the boy playing Adam first refused the apple. Finally the boy gave in and took a bite. Members of the audience gasped and cried. All knew the world was now doomed.

Children were seen everywhere in the northern frontier. Census reports list that up to 40 percent of the village dwellers were children under the age of eighteen. By contrast census takers counted only a handful of people over seventy. The number of children would have been even higher had it not been for deaths caused by diseases. With grim regularity epidemics of measles, influenza, cholera, and smallpox swept the Spanish West. These sicknesses killed mainly children and old people, the weakest members of the communities. Families of ten children were common, but often only five or six grew to adulthood. The others died young, struck down by illness.

LEARNING THROUGH WORK

At age six or seven, boys and girls began working alongside their parents. Through work the children learned to master tasks they would perform for the rest of their lives.

Girls helped their mothers wash clothes in the river or in a hollowed-out tree trunk. Tiny girls, as young as three, sat in the backyard grinding corn for tortillas with their older sisters. The women and girls would put corn kernels onto a flat stone called a metate (muh-TAH-tee). They would then crush the kernels with a device called a mano. The mano (also the Spanish word for "hand") was a cylindrical stone that women used like a rolling pin to grind corn.

Boys in New Mexico learned to tend herds of sheep by chasing down strays and throwing stones at lurking coyotes and wolves. A boy destined to be a homebuilder was taught by his father to fashion adobe brick and to cut log beams. On the cattle ranches of Texas and California, boys became accomplished horse riders by the time they were seven years old.

Adult responsibilities started early in the Spanish West. Lessons had to be mastered during the brief childhood years. At age fifteen a boy was considered mature enough to manage a farm on his own. Girls frequently married at sixteen. Boys as young as fifteen served in the army.

Foreign travelers to the northern frontier claimed that the children they met there were courteous and unusually happy. No spoiled brats or crybabies were observed. A woman from the United States visited New Mexico in the 1800s. She bought vegetables from a six-year-old girl and wrote, "Just to see the true politeness and ease displayed by that child is

MUSIC AND DANCE: A PASSION IN THE SPANISH WEST

Dance songs at Spanish West wedding celebrations were simple and lively. Often they contained nonsense words, but the words rhymed and could be sung easily while two partygoers danced. One old song had these catchy lines:

Me gusta la leche	"Milk I like
Me gusta el cafe	Coffee I like
Pero más me gusta	But what I like most
Bailar con tu.	Is to dance with you."

truly amazing; it would put many a mother in the United States to the blush."

Unquestioned respect toward one's parents was the rule in Spanish families. In California a tradition held that a boy could not shave until his father gave permission. Sometimes that permission was not granted until the boy was twenty-one and already had a thick beard.

COURTSHIP AND MARRIAGE

Sunday was a day of relaxation for the colonists. The Sabbath Day started with Mass. After church the colonists visited the village market. The market was crowded on Sundays as vendors sold fruits, vegetables, and wood carvings. Apache Indians frequently waged war with the settlers of New Mexico, but they traded goods on Sundays. Apaches brought deer and bear meat to the village market. Usually the buyers and sellers traded goods. Only rarely were silver and gold coins used to purchase items in the market.

On Sunday evenings families gathered at the village square to stroll or to enjoy the cool of the evening. The square was an ideal place for teenage boys and girls to meet. First the boy and girl caught each other's attention by exchanging shy smiles and giggles. Direct talk between them was considered bad manners. Once touched by a girl's charms, a boy approached his father. The father discussed the situation with his wife. The parents also talked to the village priest. The girl was the last to know she was the object of all this attention.

Strict rules of courtship, inherited from Spain, were practiced on the northern frontier. The first step in the courtship process came when the parents of the boy hired the services of an *escritor*, a professional letter writer. The *escritor* wrote to the girl's parents. Always the wording of the letter was flowery and formal. A typical letter read, "Most distinguished Mr. and Mrs. ———. With fitting regard and deserved affection this note comes with the sole object of making your illustrious selves aware that our son is favorably disposed toward your pleasing daughter. He wishes to place himself under your orders and to undergo the formality of the matrimonial ceremony in order to better serve you." If the girl's family was illiterate, a priest or another *escritor* was called upon to read the letter. The letter was often kept in the girl's

Colonists in the Spanish West loved to celebrate. Parties included lots of food, wine, and lively music. Most of all, people liked to dance.

Few people in the Spanish West knew how to read or write.
When a formal letter had to be written, people went to a
professional letter writer, called an **escritor.**

family chest for generations to come.

If the bride's family agreed to the match, arrangements were usually made for a dowry, the money or property the young woman brought to the marriage. Parents provided most brides with some sort of dowry—perhaps farmland, livestock, or a few gold coins.

Finally the wedding day arrived. At last all formalities were abandoned. Wedding parties were hosted by the parents of the bride. They featured wine, musicians, and tables sagging with food. Everyone in the village was invited. Worries over expenses were cast aside. A wedding was a time for the bride's family to advertise its generosity. One California traveler in the early 1800s wrote, "I was a guest at a wedding party . . . which lasted about a week, dancing kept up all night with a company of at least one hundred men and women from the adjoining ranchos, about three hours after daylight being given to sleep, after which picnics in the woods were held during the afternoon. This program continued [until] I had become so exhausted for want of regular sleep that I was glad to escape."

SPANISH TEXAS

The Spaniards did not establish settlements in Texas until the early 1700s. When exploring the region, Spanish parties met an Indian tribe whose word for "friends" was *tejas*. The Spaniards changed the word to suit their language, and the district and later the state of Texas got their name. By 1793 Texas held about seven thousand Spanish or mestizo people. Its capital and largest town was San Antonio.

❖4❖
The Church: Foundation of the Spanish West

Hear us! Hear us! Little angels are we,
Who have come from heaven
To ask for alms,
And if we are denied,
Doors and windows we will break.
Hear us! Hear us!

—A SONG CHANTED BY CHILDREN DURING ALL SOULS' DAY.
On this holy day, when Catholics prayed for the souls of the dead,
boys and girls went door-to-door asking for treats.

CALIFORNIA, LAND OF MISSIONS

Mission priests in the northern frontier considered themselves to be soldiers of God. Like soldiers they risked their lives to perform a mission. In this case their mission was to convert Indians to Christianity. In many respects these priests were the true

Worshippers hold a service outside mission
San Miguel near Santa Fe, New Mexico.

SPANISH CALIFORNIA

Authorities in Mexico City looked upon California as an overseas province. The land route there was so difficult that the region could be supplied only by ships. To strengthen their claim to California, the Spanish tried to have more people settle in the region. Officials in Mexico City even sentenced petty criminals to emigrate there. The effort failed. By the 1820s only about six thousand Spanish settlers lived in California.

pioneers of the northern frontier. They ventured into wilderness areas long before settlers arrived.

Nowhere was the mission system more prominent than in California. The overland journey from New Spain to California was arduous and fraught with danger from Indian attack. Settlers were reluctant to go to the region because of the dangers. But priests—the soldiers of God—accepted the risk to win new souls for Christ.

In 1769 Father Junípero Serra established California's first mission church, near present-day San Diego. That church was built out of logs. Father Serra hung a bell on a tree limb to summon Indians to Mass. Over the next fifty years, priests built twenty-one mission churches in California. Each mission was constructed about a day's walk from the last. Like links on a chain, the churches stretched from San Diego north to today's San Francisco. The tiny village of San Francisco was the northern boundary of Spanish California.

At the missions priests taught Native Americans practical skills: farming, carpentry, and blacksmithing. Before receiving this training, the Indians had to be baptized into the Christian faith. All too often, however, the Indians who converted to Christianity became virtual slaves to the priests. Converts (called neophytes) were forced to live in huts or barracks

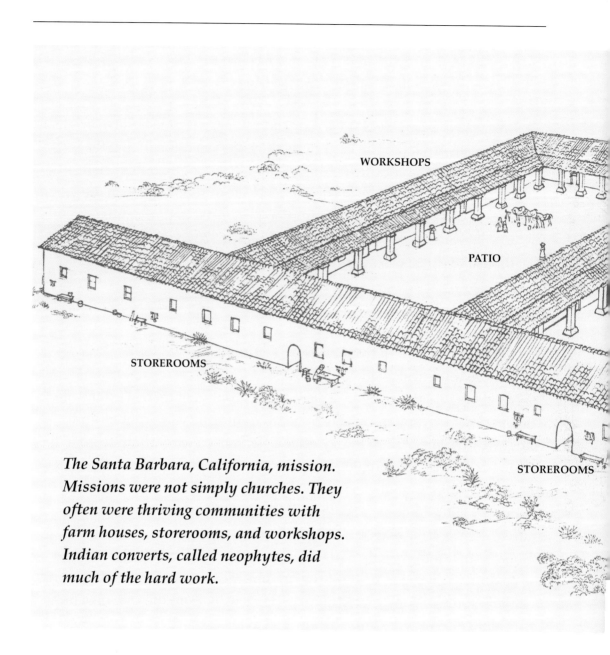

WORKSHOPS

PATIO

STOREROOMS

STOREROOMS

The Santa Barbara, California, mission. Missions were not simply churches. They often were thriving communities with farm houses, storerooms, and workshops. Indian converts, called neophytes, did much of the hard work.

near the mission church. They worked long hours in the fields or on building projects. If a neophyte attempted to escape, he was chased down by Spanish soldiers on horseback. Once captured, the runaway was tied to a post and whipped. Usually the soldiers rather than the priests did the actual whipping. That way the priests would not look cruel in the eyes of the Indians.

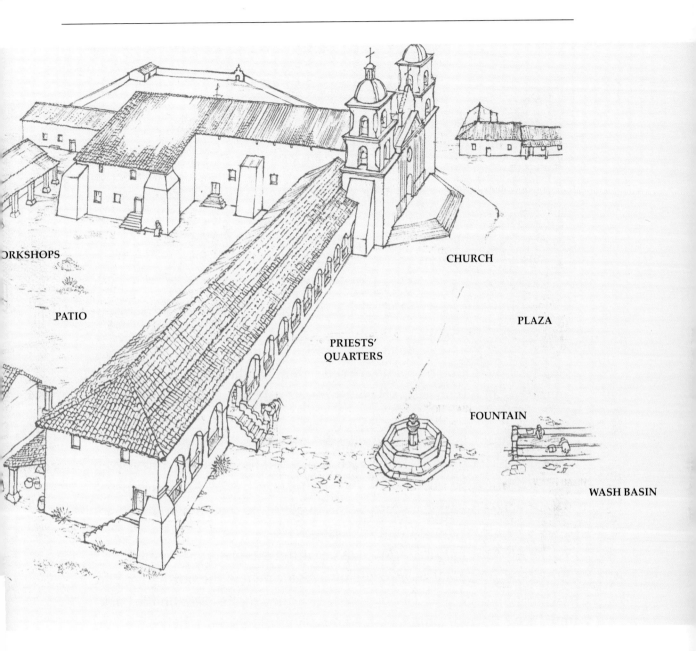

WORKSHOPS

PATIO

PRIESTS'
QUARTERS

CHURCH

PLAZA

FOUNTAIN

WASH BASIN

NEW MEXICANS CLING TO THEIR CHURCH

During the 1700s New Mexico had little contact with government authorities to the south. Left on its own, New Mexico divided roughly into two lands: an impoverished area to the north and a more comfortable region in the south.

FATHER KINO

Many priests in the Spanish West were dedicated to converting Indians through kindness, not cruelty. One such priest was Father Eusebio Francisco Kino. Accompanied only by Indian guides, he established seven missions within the borders of present-day Arizona. Father Kino respected Indian culture. For that reason he was spared while Indians of Arizona killed other black-robed priests who ventured into the region.

Poorest of the New Mexicans were the small farmers called *paisanos* (people of the soil). The *paisanos* lived in lonely villages in the north. Theirs was an untamed land, rain starved and subject to frequent attacks by fierce Apache Indians.

In the south, between Albuquerque and Santa Fe, lived the *gente de razon* (people of reason). They were also called the *ricos* (rich ones). Along the Rio Grande the *ricos* worked farms and sheep ranches. When they were attacked by Apaches, the *ricos* retreated into their thick-walled adobe houses, which became miniature forts.

The *paisanos* and *ricos* adopted very different forms of worship. During the annual Easter procession, *paisano* men of the north marched in a passionate parade. The marchers whipped themselves on the back until blood flowed. Others walked on cactus plants with their bare feet. Sometimes a man would volunteer to let his neighbors tie him to a cross. Officially the church did not approve of these rituals. But priests did little to stop the bloodletting. The *paisanos* thought that sin could be forgiven only through pain.

The *ricos* to the south practiced a gentler, happier faith. If a baby was seen smiling or giggling, the ricos said the baby was playing with angels. New Mexican *ricos* believed that saints and angels were present everywhere. One could feel them dancing among the stars at night or hear them singing with the afternoon winds.

To Roman Catholics saints are religious heroes. They are worshipped with special prayers and honored with feast days. Spanish West residents thought of saints almost as if they were family members. San Isidro was the favorite saint among farmers. Paintings show him driving a wooden plow pulled by an angel. New Mexican farm families prayed for rain and healthy crops in front of a statue of San Isidro. If the saint failed to deliver, he was punished. His statue was locked inside the family trunk.

The people of Santa Fe venerated a wooden statue called Our Lady of the Rosary, the Conqueror. The statue, about twenty-eight inches tall, was brought from Mexico in the early 1600s. It was believed to have given the people of Santa Fe strength to triumph during a terrible period of Indian warfare in the 1680s. Ever since that time, Our Lady of the Rosary, the Conqueror was worshipped almost like a saint. Her statue still exists. It stands in the chapel of Santa Fe's Cathedral of Saint Francis. During Corpus Christi Day, in early summer, it is paraded

Paisanos *practiced painful forms of worship. Here they walk on cactus plants, believing that only by such suffering could their sins be forgiven.*

through the streets on a special float. The Lady, however, is no longer called the Conqueror. Today "the Conqueror" has been changed to "the Unifier," and the Lady is hailed as a princess of peace.

A picture falling off the wall for no reason was a sign that a witch had entered the home. The sudden death of a pet cat or dog was also proof of witchcraft. Witches (*brujas*) could be either men or women, but women were most frequently suspected. Any unusual behavior on the part of a woman could lead to a finger-pointing accusation of contact with the devil. A New Mexican servant girl once told a judge that she saw the woman of the house laughing while reading a book. This, said the servant, was proof of witchcraft. Women in the Spanish West rarely read. Laughing at a book was very strange behavior indeed.

Looking at a neighbor in an odd way meant that one was casting the evil eye (*mal de ojo*). Mothers often pulled their babies away from admiring strangers. The mothers feared the evil eye would cause the baby to get sick.

Even animals could become possessed by evil spirits. An owl following a sheepherder home was a wicked sign. Owls sometimes did evil deeds

FATE AND FAITH

Her voice was so eerie it could turn a brave man to stone. If she was heard crying on a doorstep at night, death would surely visit the household. She was La Llorona, "the Crying Woman." La Llorona was a spirit who haunted towns in Mexico. The belief in her chilling powers was taken north to the frontier. Some stories said she searched for her lost children, crying out to them. Other stories claimed La Llorona had murdered her children and now cried in the night out of grief and guilt. Compelling belief in spirits and witches held sway in all parts of the northern frontier for witches. A New Mexican red-bellied snake, called a whip snake, had devilish powers. According to stories, the whip snake could stand on its tail and lash the backs of farmers trying to work in the fields. The whip snake also stole milk from nursing mothers. The snake sucked on the mother's breast while she was sleeping and kept the baby pacified by putting its tail in the baby's mouth.

Our Lady of the Rosary, the Conqueror, was the most honored statue in the Spanish West. The statue still exists and is kept in Santa Fe's Cathedral of Saint Francis.

Belief in a mythical creature called the water dog was widespread, especially among children. The water dog, it was said, delighted in biting young New Mexican girls swimming in the Rio Grande. If a boy wanted to frighten girls bathing in the river, he sneaked up on them and shouted, "Water dog!" The girls scattered.

Not all people with spiritual powers were evil. A *curandera,* a person believed to have healing powers, used magical forces and folk medicine to perform good works. Most *curanderas* were women. They stopped bleeding by placing cobwebs on a cut. They treated a person with epilepsy by rubbing a newborn pig on the patient's forehead. Baked badger meat in magpie soup was the *curandera*'s prescription for asthma. Oils from skunks or coyotes were given to older people suffering from rheumatism. A *curandera* was able to thwart the power of an evil witch by ringing her house with a circle of salt. Even a young man hoping to win the heart of a woman went to the *curandera* for help. The *curandera* placed the bone of a jackrabbit in the woman's coffee, and thus opened her vision to the man's virtues.

☙5☙
The Spanish West Community

"Having received an order for the construction of quarters for the presidial company of this Province, it is desired that those persons who have no land to sow this year shall take part in the work."

—AN ORDER WRITTEN BY THE GOVERNOR OF NEW MEXICO IN 1789.
The order directs all farmers who have no pressing duties on their farms to help build a new army barracks. These types of community projects were common enterprises in New Spain's northern frontier.

COMMUNITIES AT WORK

In the parched lands of New Mexico, farmers regarded water as a favor granted or withheld by God. Farmers took figures of saints into the fields. They pointed the figures to the sky and begged them to produce rain. If days went by without rain, the farmers shook the saints' statues to demand their attention. At home they stood the statues upside down to remind the saints of their duties.

When rains finally filled the streams, the community sprang into action. Conserving and distributing water was vital for survival in colonial New Mexico.

A complex network of irrigation ditches, dug by the people, brought water from the streams to the fields. Farmers often planted cotton-wood trees along the sides of the main ditch that fed their village. The trees shaded the irrigation water, diminishing evaporation. The village appointed a team of three or four men to open and shut gates on the main irrigation ditch. In this manner water was channeled to family plots, where corn and beans were planted.

A vaquero thunders across the ranch, sending out his lasso to catch a steer.

COWBOY LINGO

The word *lariat* comes from the Spanish words *la reata*, meaning "the rope." *Lasso* derives from the Spanish *lazo*, a "noose" or "snare." Cowboys who later came from the United States to work on ranches in Texas and New Mexico borrowed many Spanish terms. The cowboys herded cattle into a fenced-in pen, a corral, whose name comes from a Spanish word of the same spelling. A cowboy who knew his job well was said to be savvy, derived from *saber*, "to know." These imported words made up the colorful cowboy lingo; *lingo* is rooted in *lengua*, or "tongue."

Most often the team distributed the water fairly. But when rain was scarce, fights broke out. Murders even took place over water rights. Many villages had a special court of older men that dealt only with water allotment cases.

Spanish Texas was cattle country. Colonists brought a breed of Spanish cattle there, and the animals thrived on the rich grasslands. Over the decades they became the Texas longhorns, later made famous by writers portraying the Wild West. Entire communities in Texas pitched in to work at roundup time. The most important workers were the cowboys, called *vaqueros* (vah-KEHR-ohs). Many *vaqueros* were Indians who were taught riding skills by missionary priests. They amazed their instructors. A *vaquero* could ride all day without tiring. With his rawhide lariat he could rope cattle as far as one hundred feet away.

California too was devoted to cattle raising. At work a "Californio" rancher spent days at a time on horseback. It could be said that the Californios of old were as attached to their horses as today's Californians are to their cars. The Californios were so devoted to cattle and horses that they ignored an abundant food resource right at their front door—the fish in the sea. Rarely did the people of Spanish California eat fish. Why? A

Native Americans of the Spanish West never stopped worshipping their own gods and spirits. Here an entire village joins in the Sunset Dance, a ceremony in honor of the evening sun.

traveler from the United States once said, "If [the Californios] could go to sea on their horses and fish from their saddles, they would.... But to sit quietly in a boat is for them entirely too tame a business."

New Mexicans raised sheep rather than cattle because it was more difficult for Indian raiders to ride away with sheep herds. Indian attack was a constant threat for New Mexicans. Wars with Native Americans persisted despite efforts in both communities to live in peace.

COOPERATION AND CONFLICT

When Spanish colonists entered New Mexico, they found some Indian tribes living in small farming villages while others were nomadic. They called the village dwellers Pueblos, after the Spanish word for "village" or "town." From the start the colonists established close ties with many Pueblo groups. The nomads, however, remained unfriendly with the settlers.

By the year 1680 Spanish settlement in New Mexico was well established. The capital city of Santa Fe held about 2,500 colonists. In the countryside Spanish farmers lived in peace with their Pueblo neighbors. Most of New Mexico's Pueblos had accepted Christianity. Yet they insisted on tribal dancing and worshipping their old gods. The Pueblos believed in the existence of many gods and spirits. They simply added the Christian god to their already long list of deities. This practice infuriated Spanish priests. The priests ordered soldiers to capture those Pueblos caught dancing or praying to spirits. The Indians were then jailed, whipped, or even hanged.

Led by a chief named Popé, the Pueblos revolted against the Spaniards. In the countryside Pueblo warriors burned churches and slaughtered priests and settlers. During the late summer of 1680, the Pueblos captured their biggest prize—the city of Santa Fe. Surviving residents of the capital fled over desert land to what is now El Paso, Texas. Many died en route.

During the terrible journey to Texas, the colonists carried the statue of Our Lady of the Rosary, the Conqueror. Fervently, they prayed to the image for the return of their homes, now occupied by Indians. Twelve years later the colonists and a unit of Spanish soldiers marched back to Santa Fe. By this time the Pueblo rebels had lost their will to fight. The reconquest of the city was bloodless. New Mexicans concluded that Our Lady of the Rosary, the Conqueror had answered their prayers. Forever afterward the image was loved as a messenger from God.

After the Pueblo Revolt of 1680, the Pueblos and the colonists lived in relative peace. In fact, the Pueblos and the Spaniards often fought side

WHAT'S IN A WORD?

In the Southwest today the word *pueblo* has three meanings: First, it is a town. Second, it is a group of Indian tribes. Third, it is a multistoried community dwelling once inhabited by the Indians of the Southwest. To further complicate this definition, the Indian people referred to as Pueblos are really members of several distinct tribes. Each tribe has its own customs and language.

Inside of a Pueblo Indian house.

by side against a common enemy—the nomadic tribes. The nomads, principally the Navajos and the Apaches, waged constant hit-and-run battles with the settlers. Colonists slept uneasily at night. Farmers working the fields looked over their shoulder a dozen times during the course of the day. Deadly attack could come at any time and from any direction.

With their Pueblo neighbors, however, the colonists readily integrated. Spaniards frequently married Pueblo Indians. Curiously, marriage preferences were based on class, not on race. Wealthy Spaniards wanted their sons or daughters to marry only the offspring of tribal chiefs. Intermarriage was so widespread that people of wholly Spanish blood practically disappeared by the 1800s. By then the vast majority of colonists were mestizos.

In addition to intermarriage, the Indians and Spanish settlers traded goods with each other and attended church services together. Often the Spaniards made friendly gestures toward the nomadic tribes. Apache horsemen, for example, hired by the government of New Spain, delivered mail to the far-flung settlements.

Still, bloody warfare erupted. Certainly the Spanish insistence that Indians worship only the Christian God was an underlying cause of the conflicts. The Indians, especially the nomads, refused to abandon their beliefs in a host of gods and spirits. Native Americans, in fact, were often confused by the Spanish religious custom of praying to numerous saints. They would tell the Spaniards that this custom was evidence that they also worshipped many gods.

TRADING GOODS: EXCITEMENT IN A LONELY LAND

"The general eagerness found among New Mexicans for commerce with the neighboring states is certainly astonishing," wrote a Spanish official named Antonio Barriero. Isolation from neighboring people plagued New Mexico. Commerce—the trading of goods with other communities—was a welcome break from that isolation.

All New Mexicans looked forward to attending the annual trade fair

NAVAJO BLANKETS, A TREASURE OF THE FRONTIER

The Spaniards taught the Navajos how to shear sheep, spin the wool into yarn, and create blankets by weaving the yarn on a loom. The Navajos soon outdid their teachers. Navajo craftspeople used dyes from local plants to give their woolen products blazing colors. Those same dyes had once decorated Navajo deerskin clothing. Blankets and serapes made by Navajo weavers brought high prices at trade fairs.

held in the northern Mexican city of Chihuahua. Going to the fair meant a two-month trip, much of it over mountains and deserts. Yet every year thousands of settlers trekked south for the two-week extravaganza. They traveled in a huge procession made up of creaking oxcarts, scampering dogs, and herds of horses and sheep. This grand parade began in northern New Mexico and picked up followers as it wound south. Entire families made the journey. Traveling in such a large group provided safety from Indian attack. Also the crowd itself was part of the fun. At night hundreds of campfires burned. Singing, dancing, and storytelling enthralled the people.

At the Chihuahua fairgrounds New Mexicans ogled goods rarely seen in their remote province—perfumes, fine jewelry, stationery, gloves, fancy hats, elegant suits and dresses, and stockings. Only on occasion was money exchanged at the fair. Mostly goods were traded. The New Mexicans traded sheep, horses, woolen blankets, buffalo robes, leather products, and pine nuts. More important than the trading was the chance to meet new people. The fair was attended by as many as 50,000 citizens of New Spain. For the colonists of lonely New Mexico, this many people gathered in one town amounted to a wild party.

Residents of California were also eager to trade goods. But the Californios let the traders come to them. California port towns such as San Diego and Monterey buzzed with excitement when a foreign ship arrived. Everyone came to see what goods the ships had to sell. Richard Henry Dana, a sailor from Massachusetts, blamed the people's "laziness" for their reliance on articles made in other countries. "The Californians are an idle, thriftless people, and can make nothing for themselves," wrote Dana in his classic book Two Years before the Mast. "The country abounds in grapes, yet they buy bad wines made in Boston." Dana concluded that California's pleasant climate and fertile soil had spoiled its citizens.

ARIZONA

Arizona was the least-developed region of the Spanish West. Unforgiving deserts and hostile Native Americans discouraged Spanish colonists from immigrating to Arizona. The only settlement was at Tucson, and that was more a fort than it was a town.

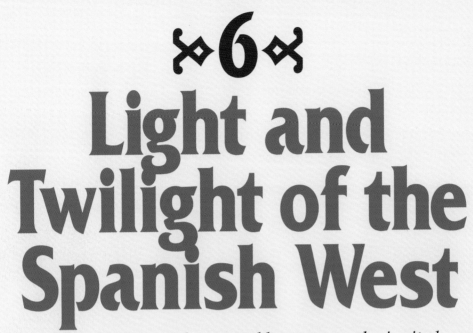

❖6❖
Light and Twilight of the Spanish West

"We were frequently stopped by women who invited us into their houses to eat; in every place we halted there was a contest [as to] who should be our host."

—THE UNITED STATES ARMY OFFICER ZEBULON PIKE,
who commented on the overwhelming friendliness of the New Mexican people he met during a visit in 1806

THE SPANISH WEST PERSONALITY

There were no poorhouses or orphanages in the Spanish West. A child left alone due to the death of parents was quickly adopted. Destitute or sick people were taken into households. The finest room in most houses was the one reserved for guests.

The annual *posada* (puh-SAH-duh), the Christmas pageant, celebrated the people's kindness. The posada (*posada* means "inn" in Spanish) was a procession that re-enacted the plight of Joseph and Mary as they searched for an inn. Holding candles, a group of villagers went from house to house singing, "Who will give lodging to we pilgrims / Who are tired of traveling on the road?" Graciously all families opened their doors to the singers—all but one. Custom demanded that one house be designated as the devil's lair. In a spiteful voice the man playing the devil sang out, "We do not give lodging, for we cannot serve / Those who may be thieves

Children still walk in the annual **posada,** *or Christmas pageant, in San Antonio, Texas.*

Spanish West colonists say prayers for the dead on All Souls' Day.

coming here to rob." The lesson of the posada was clear. Only the devil is distrustful of strangers. Only the devil would turn away a hungry and tired traveler.

There was a reverse side to the Spanish West personality. Visitors often condemned the people for their "passions," meaning their fiery tempers. Men carried knives on their belts as farm tools. When an argument broke out, the knives served as deadly weapons. Wearing guns in holsters was common because of the threat of Indian attack. The practice also meant that fights were often settled by gunfire. Men argued over women and over gambling. They argued when they got drunk on locally produced brandy. A man calling another man a coward or a liar was demanding a fight. In the Spanish West a fight to the death was frequently thought of as "an affair of honor" rather than a murder.

FIESTA!

Fiesta is a Spanish word for "party." In the Spanish West this often meant a party thrown by an entire village. Community calendars were dotted with festival days. New Mexican villages held fiestas at sheepshearing time. Texas towns celebrated the end of a cattle roundup. About half the festivals were hosted by the church. Religious celebrations included Easter, Christmas, All Souls' Day (when relatives honored their dead), and many, many saint's days.

Villages rocked with music at fiesta time. The guitar was a favorite instrument, followed by the violin and the mandolin. Rarely was a Spanish West crowd content to simply listen to a group of players or to a solo singer. They were a singing people, and burst into song at the opening note.

Sports and games were a highlight of the fiestas. Californios demonstrated their horsemanship by racing their animals at breakneck speed and then bending low to scoop up a small silver coin that had been placed on the ground. In Texas teams mounted on horses played a game similar to football. Members of one team advanced a watermelon by handing it off to one another while the opposing team tried to snatch the watermelon away.

Sadly, some of the games involved cruelty to animals. Cockfights were staged from California to Texas. The cockfights were held in an open pit, around which spectators formed a ring to watch the gory action. In the pit two gamecocks (fighting roosters with razor-sharp metal spurs attached to their claws) tore at each other until one was killed. Californios also amused themselves by chaining a bull and a grizzly bear together and goading them to fight.

SINGING LOS ANGELES

Los Angeles, California, was a tiny Spanish village in the early 1800s. But it was a village of singers. It is said that the villagers had an interesting custom. The first person to rise and begin work in the morning was supposed to start singing a song. The next person up and about was required to join the first. By sunrise, when everyone was out of bed, all the voices of Los Angeles were joined in a single song.

Cockfights were popular from California to Texas. People did not seem to consider that they involved cruelty to animals.

Gambling was heavy during these so-called sporting activities. In New Mexico, where few people had cash, men bet farm animals and property. Entire farms and herds of valuable livestock could be lost in an evening.

No matter what they did at the fiesta, men and women enjoyed dressing up. Ladies wore their best party dresses. Handheld fans became a woman's instrument of expression. A laughing woman fluttered the fan gently in front of her face. A woman arguing pointed the fan furiously at her opponent as if it were a sword. But the men were the true dandies of the fiestas. They delighted in wearing wide-brimmed hats and cloth jackets alive with stripes and colorful patterns.

Nothing excited the festival-loving Spanish West residents more than dances. In a large town such as Santa Fe, a fandango (a Spanish word for a public dance) was held somewhere every night. A United States visitor said of the fandangos, "From the gravest priest to the buffoon, from the

THE SANTA FE TRAIL

Winding from Independence in present-day Missouri to Santa Fe, New Mexico, the eight-hundred-mile Santa Fe Trail was an early link between the Spanish West and the United States. William Becknell, an Anglo-American trader, first used the trail in 1821. Becknell hauled oil lamps and farm tools to Santa Fe on ox-drawn wagons and exchanged them for New Mexican woolen products. Soon dozens of other trading caravans used the trail, much to the delight of the commerce-loving New Mexicans.

richest nabob to the beggar . . . all partake of this exhilarating amusement." The visitor went on to say that even jail inmates were released from their cells during popular fandangos. This was not done out of sympathy for the prisoners. Instead, the inmates were let go because the jail guards wanted to attend the dances.

TWILIGHT OF THE SPANISH WEST

From 1810 to 1821 Mexican patriots fought a war of independence against Spain. The patriots triumphed and formed the Mexican nation. After three hundred years New Spain was no more. An independent Mexico now ruled the northern frontier. Under the new government the church lost some of its power. Missions in California were forced to sell much of their land to ranchers. But the change in government from New Spain to Mexico had little impact on most residents of the far-flung regions of the frontier.

The end of the Spanish West came ultimately at the hands of the United States. For years English-speaking Americans of the United States had pushed relentlessly westward. Eventually these Anglo Americans came to believe that they had a special right to expand their territory. They were guided by a belief known as Manifest Destiny. The spirit of Manifest Destiny told the Anglo Americans that it was their fate—indeed, it was the will of God—that their country expand from the Atlantic to the Pacific Ocean. Mexico's northern frontier blocked the westward path. This situation invited war.

The troubles began in Texas. In 1821 Stephen Austin had led a small party of settlers from the United States to Texas, where they raised cattle. Within ten years nearly 30,000 United States immigrants lived in Texas. The Anglo Americans, who called themselves Texans, broke away from Mexico and declared Texas to be an independent nation. In 1836 a terrible battle was fought at the Alamo in San Antonio. The Alamo was an old Spanish church that the Anglo Americans had turned into a fort. About 180 Texans were killed by the Mexican army at the Alamo.

The bloody Battle of the Alamo enraged people in the United States. The Texas issue, combined with the spirit of Manifest Destiny, triggered a war between the United States and Mexico. The war was fought from 1846 to 1848. As a result of the war, Mexico lost the vast territories of its northern frontier to the ever-expanding United States.

SLAVERY AND THE TEXANS

It is often said that the Texans broke away from the Mexican government in order to achieve their freedom. In the minds of the Texans, this was probably the case. But what about their slaves? Many Texans had emigrated from Kentucky and Tennessee, states that allowed slavery. Some had brought slaves to the new land. The Mexican government forbade slavery and was pressuring the Texans to set their slaves free. Ironically, one of the "freedoms" the Texans fought for was their freedom to own slaves.

A view of the rugged but beautiful land of New Mexico.

California was a particularly bitter loss for Mexico. The year the war ended, a ranch foreman discovered specks of gold in a California stream, and the find triggered the great Gold Rush. In just three years, once-sleepy California became a booming region with a population nearing 100,000.

The Mexican-American War ushered in the last transition of the Spanish West. The region began as the northern frontier of New Spain, became the northern frontier of Mexico, and finally evolved into the southwestern section of the United States. The 40,000 or so Mexican residents of the old Spanish West became United States citizens. Their descendants today are residents of New Mexico, Texas, Arizona, and California.

The Spanish West changed, but never really died. The Spaniards were the first Europeans to see the western lands, and they gave its features names that have lasted over the centuries: the mountains of the Sierra Madre, the Rio Grande, and the Pecos River. To this day, only the Spanish word mesa can properly describe the flat-topped hills so common in the Southwest. Beyond words and place names, the pioneers from Mexico developed a special way of life on a special land. The Spanish West belonged to a powerful period in history, a time that shaped the future of the United States.

Glossary

adobe: A sun-dried clay brick once used widely to build houses in the Southwest.

allotment: A distribution or share of something.

buffoon: A foolish person; a clown.

Californio: A resident of California in the Spanish West era.

conquistador: One of many hundreds of Spaniards who came to the Americas in the 1500s and conquered the native people there.

dapper: Very stylishly dressed.

deity: A god or powerful spirit.

enthrall: To fascinate.

fandango: A public dance in Spanish countries; the word *fandango* is also used to describe a fast dance, in triple time.

fraught: Filled with.

gala: Festive.

heirloom: A precious object passed down from one generation to another.

lair: The dwelling of a dangerous animal or spirit.

lingo: The special language or words of the cowboys, lingo comes from the Spanish word *lengua* ("tongue" or "form of speech").

Manifest Destiny: The belief, popular in the first half of the 1800s, that the United States was destined, or fated, to expand its borders from the Atlantic to the Pacific Ocean.

Mass: A Roman Catholic church service.

mestizo (meh-STEE-zoh): A person of mixed Spanish and Native American ancestry.

nabob: A wealthy person.

nomadic: Wandering; having no permanent home.

ogle: To look at longingly.

pantomime: Telling a story through gestures, without words.

plunder: To take by force.

serape (suh-RAH-pee): A heavy woolen shawl, worn as a cloak or used as a blanket.

staple: A product or crop such as grain that serves as the basis of a people's diet.

thwart: To block a process.

trek: To go on a journey.

vendor: A seller of goods.

The Spanish West in Time

1519–1521—Spaniards conquer the Aztec capital (now Mexico City) and establish the empire of New Spain.

1540–42—The Spaniard Francisco Vásquez de Coronado explores the far northern region of New Spain. Coronado's scouting parties trek over what are now New Mexico, Texas, Oklahoma, Kansas, Arizona, Colorado, and California.

1598—Juan de Oñate establishes San Juan in present-day New Mexico. It is the first permanent settlement in New Spain's northern frontier.

1610—Pedro de Peralta founds the town of Santa Fe as New Mexico's capital.

1680—During the great Pueblo Revolt, the Indian leader Popé drives Spanish settlers from Santa Fe.

1692—Spanish colonists reconquer Santa Fe.

1700—Father Eusebio Francisco Kino establishes Mission San Xavier del Bac near Tucson, Arizona.

1718—Spanish colonists build Mission San Antonio de Valero (later called the Alamo) in San Antonio, Texas.

1769—Father Junípero Serra constructs California's first mission church at present-day San Diego.

1781—The colonial town of Los Angeles, California, is founded.

1806—The United States Army officer Zebulon Pike enters New Mexico from the north, on a mission of exploration to study western lands and report his findings to his government.

1821—In Mexico patriots overthrow the government of New Spain and Mexico becomes an independent nation.

1836—United States immigrants living in Texas declare themselves independent from Mexico, and a terrible battle is fought at the Alamo.

1846—Mexico and the United States go to war.

1848—The Mexican-American War concludes. Mexico cedes its northern frontier to the United States. What was once the Spanish West becomes California and the American Southwest.

Places to Visit

ARIZONA

Highway 666:

This state highway is also called the Coronado Trail. A scenic route, it runs over deserts and through forests, and climbs rugged mountains. The roadway roughly follows the route taken by the Spanish explorer Francisco Vásquez de Coronado in the 1540s.

Mission San Xavier del Bac (near Tucson):

The dedicated Spanish priest Eusebio Francisco Kino built the first mission church here in 1700. The church was rebuilt several times and today is hailed as one of the finest of all Spanish-style churches still standing in the United States.

CALIFORNIA

Highway 1:

A pathway called the Camino Real (Royal Road) connected California's twenty-one mission churches. The pathway hugged the ocean and stretched from San Diego north to Yerba Buena (present-day San Francisco). Today's California Route 1 runs along the same path as the old Camino Real.

Missions:

The twenty-one California mission churches built by Spanish and Mexican priests can be visited today. Mission San Juan Capistrano is famous for the swallows that return there every spring. Mission San Luis Rey de Francia (near Oceanside) is one of the largest and most beautiful in the state.

NEW MEXICO

Albuquerque:

Visitors to the Old Town section of Albuquerque walk along narrow, twisting streets lined with three-hundred-year-old adobe houses. In the heart of Old Town stands the San Felipe de Neri Church, built in 1706.

El Morro (also called Inscription Rock):

For hundreds of years travelers chiseled their names, dates, and other messages on the face of this huge sandstone cliff, which rises near the city of Grants. Oldest of the inscriptions (dated April 1605) is that of Juan de Oñate. Oñate is considered to be the founder of Spanish New Mexico.

Santa Fe:

Santa Fe was the capital of Spanish New Mexico and Mexican New Mexico, and it is now the capital of the American state. The city's historic plaza was first laid out in 1610. Over the years it held events ranging from bullfights to fandangos. The plaza was a battleground during the Pueblo Revolt of 1680. The Palace of the Governors, on the plaza, is the oldest public building in the United States. The History Museum of the Palace of the Governors displays furniture, clothing, and housewares of Spanish New Mexico. About a block east of the plaza is the Cathedral of Saint Francis, where the statue of Our Lady of the Rosary, the Unifier can be seen. Beyond Saint Francis is the San Miguel Mission, built in 1636. It is the oldest church still in use in the United States.

Taos:

More than seven hundred years ago, Pueblo Indians settled in Taos. Beginning in the 1600s Spanish missionary priests moved in with the Native Americans. Taos later became home to traders from the United States, including the famous Kit Carson. Later still, artists from many lands set up residence there. As a result of these influences, Taos holds a magical collection of art and architecture that spans the ages.

TEXAS

The Alamo:

In the heart of San Antonio, the Alamo was built in 1718 to serve as a Spanish mission church. During the famous 1836 battle, the entire Texas force of some 180 soldiers was killed at the Alamo. Paintings and models of the battle as well as historical objects are displayed there today.

La Villita:

Located in San Antonio, La Villita is a restored early Texas town filled with colorful houses in the Spanish style.

Mission San Jose: This mission church in San Antonio, built in 1720, is a splendid example of Spanish architecture.

To Learn More...

BOOKS

Altman, Linda Jacobs. *California.* Celebrate the States Series. New York: Marshall Cavendish, 1997.

Anderson, Joan. *Spanish Pioneers of the Southwest.* New York: Lodestar Books, Dutton Children's Books, 1989.

Aylesworth, Thomas, and Virginia Aylesworth. *The Southwest: Texas, New Mexico, California.* New York: Chelsea House, 1988.

Bredeson, Carmen. *Texas. Celebrate the States Series.* New York: Marshall Cavendish, 1997.

Lasky, Kathrin. *Days of the Dead.* New York: Hyperion, 1994.

Pinchot, Jane. *The Mexicans in America.* Milwaukee: Lerner, 1989.

Stein, R. Conrad. *Fransicisco de Coronado.* World's Great Explorer Series. Chicago: Children's Press, 1992.

————. *New Mexico.* America the Beautiful Series. Chicago: Children's Press, 1988.

Weisberg, Barbara. *Coronado's Golden Quest.* Milwaukee: Raintree Steck-Vaughn, 1993.

AUDIO AND VIDEO

Three Worlds Meet, a 35-minute video that covers early Native American history through the Spanish conquest, grades 5-12. Schlessinger Video Productions, Bala Cynwyd, PA, 1996.

Five Hundred Nations, Cassette #3 of *Clash of Cultures: The People Who Met Columbus.* 50 minutes. Warner Home Video, Burbank, CA, 1995.

WEBSITES*

http://www.calhist.org/ A website sponsored by the California Historical Society of San Francisco (the state's official historical society). Covers many aspects of California history including the Gold Rush and the Spanish periods.

http://www.tsha.utexas.edu/history-onlineindex.htmc Entitled *Texas History Online from the Texas State Historical Association,* this website has colorful pictures and allows viewers to click on pages about the Indian and the Spanish eras of Texas history.

Websites change from time to time. For additional on-line information, check with your media specialist at your local library.

Bibliography

Campa, Arthur L. *Hispanic Culture in the Southwest.* Norman, OK: University of Oklahoma Press, 1979.

Dana, Richard Henry. *Two Years before the Mast.* Danbury, CT: Grolier/Harvard Classics, 1980.

Daniels, George C., ed. *The Spanish West.* New York: Time-Life Books, 1976.

Fehrenbach, T. R. *Lone Star, A History of Texas and the Texans.* Avenal, NJ: Random House Value, 1991.

Hallenbeck, Cleve. *Land of the Conquistadors.* Caldwell, ID: Caxton Press, 1950.

Jackson, Donald, ed. *The Journals of Zebulon Pike.* Norman, OK: University of Oklahoma Press, 1966.

Jones, Oakah, Jr. *Los Paisanos* (Spanish settlers on the northern frontier of New Spain). Norman, OK: University of Oklahoma Press, 1979.

Otero-Warren, Nina. *Old Spain in Our Southwest.* Chicago, IL: Rio Grande Press, 1962; first published by Harcourt Brace, 1936.

Pamphlets and papers from the History Museum of the Palace of the Governors in Santa Fe, New Mexico.

Watkins, T. H. *California, An Illustrated History.* Palo Alto, CA: American West Publishing Co., 1973.

Weber, David J. *The Mexican Frontier, 1821-1846: the American Southwest under Mexico.* Albuquerque, NM: University of New Mexico Press, 1982.

Notes on Quotes

The quotations from this book are from the following sources:

The Spanish West: New Spain's Northern Frontier
Page 9, "It is no doubt": Daniels, *The Spanish West*, p. 7.

Life and Work in a Lonely Land
Page 15, "The region farthest north": History Museum.

Page 20, "Here corn is God": History Museum.

Page 23, "We were of the poor": Fehrenbach, *Lone Star*, p. 57.

Growing Up in the Spanish West
Page 25, "The Hummingbird tells me": Otero-Warren, *Old Spain*, p. 116.

Page 28, "Just to see the true": Hallenbeck, *Land of the Conquistadors*, p. 327.

Page 30, "Most distinguished Mr. and Mrs": *Old Spain*, p. 40.

Page 33, "I was a guest": Daniels, *The Spanish West*, p. 170.

The Church: Foundation of the Spanish West
Page 35, "Hear us! Hear us!": *Old Spain*, p. 72.

The Spanish West Community
Page 45, "Having received an order": History Museum.

Page 48, "If [the Californios] could go to sea": *The Spanish West*, p. 173.

Page 51, "The general eagerness": Hallenbeck, *Land of the Conquistadors*, p. 303.

Page 53, "The Californians are an idle": Dana, *Two Years before the Mast*, p. 77.

Light and Twilight of the Spanish West
Page 55, "We were frequently": Jackson, *The Journals of Zebulon Pike*, p. 242.

Page 56, "Who will give" and "We do not give": Campa, *Hispanic Culture in the Southwest*, p. 229.

Page 59, "From the gravest priest": *The Spanish West*, p. 136.

Index

Page numbers for illustrations are in boldface

Alamo, the, 61
animals, 42–43, 58, **59**
Arizona, 6, 11, 40, 53
Austin, Stephen, 61

banco, 19
Barriero, Antonio, 51
Becknell, William, 60

Cabeza de Vaca, 9
California, 6, 10, 29
    cattle raising, 28, 47
    cattle ranches of, 28
    Gold Rush, 62
    missions, 36–39, **36, 38–39**, 60
    singing Los Angeles, 58
    Spanish, 37
    trading goods, 53
    wedding party, 33
cattle, 28, 47
children of the Spanish West
    in annual posada, **56**
    courtship and marriage, 29–33
    education, 26–28, **26**
    learning through work, 28–29
church, the
    California missions, 36–39, **36, 38–39**
    church design, 19
    fiesta and religious celebrations, **57**, 58
    New Mexicans, 39–43, **41**
    religious beliefs, 26–27
clothing of the Spanish West, 22–23
community, Spanish West
    communities at work, 46–48
    cooperation and conflict, 49, 51

trading goods, 51–53
Coronado, Francisco Vásquez de, 11
courtship and marriage, 29–33
cowboys, 47
craftsmen, 19–20, **19**
curandera, 43

Dana, Richard Henry, 53
dance, 10, 29, **30–31**, 59–60
dowry, 33

escritor, 30, 32

fandango, 10, 59–60
farmers, 10, 46, 51
fiesta, 57–60
fish, 47–48
food, 10, 20–22

gambling, 59
gente de razon, 40
Grand Canyon, 11, **11**

Holy Communion, first, 27
homes in the Spanish West
    adobe houses, 16–20, **16, 18**
    clothing, 22–23
    cooking, 20–22

iron, 20

Kino, Father Eusebio Francisco, 40

La Llorona ("the Crying Woman"), 42
language, Spanish and Indian, 10
lariat, 47

Manifest Destiny, 61
mano, 28
marriage, 29–33
mesa, 62
mestizos, 16–17, 33, 51
metate, 28
Mexican–American War, 60–62
Mexico
        New Spain, 12–13
missions, 36–39, **36**, **38–39**, 60
music and dance, 29, **30–31**, 58
mythical creatures, 43

Native Americans of the Spanish West
        Apache Indians, 29, 40
        Aztec Indians, 10, 11
        children, 27
        conversion to Christianity, 37–38, 49, 51
        gods and spirits, **48**
        homes of, **16**, 17
        intermarriage between Spaniards and,
                10, 16, 51
        Navajo blankets, 52
        Pueblo Indians, 49, **50**, 51
        Spanish colonists and, 10
        wars between Spaniards and, 13, 48, 49
neophytes, 37–38
New Mexico, 6, **62**
        arrival of Spanish colonists in, 10, 13, 23, 49
        children, 28–29
        Coronado's exploration of, 11
        mission, **36**
        New Mexicans and the church, 39–43, **41**
        Santa Fe Trail, 60
        sheep raising, 48
        trading goods, 51–52
New Spain, 12–13

Oñate, Juan de, 23
Our Lady of the Rosary, the Conqueror,
        41–42, **43**, 49

paisanos, 40, **41**
Pike, Zebulon, 55
posada, 56–57, **56**
priests, 26, 27, 36–37
pueblo, defined, 50
Pueblo Indians, 49, **50**, 51

rebozo, 22
ricos, 40–41

saints, 41, 46
San Isidro, saint, 41
santeros, 19, 20
serape, 22
Serra, Junípero, 37
sheep, 48
sickness, 28
singing, 58
slavery, 61
Spanish West,
        arrival of Spanish colonists in, 6, 10, 13
        Spanish horsemen, **6–7**
        Spanish settlers as America's first
                pioneers, 6
        twilight of the, 60–62
spiritual powers, 42–43
sports and games, 58, **59**
storms, 13

Texas, 6, 28, 33, 47, 61
trade, 51–53

vaqueros, **46**, 47
vigas, 17

water conservation, 46–47
witches, 42, 43
women of the Spanish West
        cooking, 20–22
        handheld fans, 59
        maintenance of adobe homes, 17

About the Author

Conrad Stein was born and grew up in Chicago. After serving in the United States Marines, he attended the University of Illinois and graduated with a degree in history. Mr. Stein lived in Mexico for seven years. Mexican history and culture have always fascinated him. The author also lived briefly in New Mexico, where he was overwhelmed by the beauty of the Southwest. Mr. Stein is a full-time writer. He has published more than eighty books for young readers. He now lives in Chicago with his wife, children's book author Deborah Kent, and their daughter, Janna.